BOOK SIMULATOR

The Reader's Guide to Not Reading

Book Simulator: Print Edition
by Chris Yee

ISBN 978-0-9973536-8-6

Published by To The Moon Publishing
www.nerdchomp.com/tothemoonpublishing

YOU CHOSE PRINT

Hello. Thank you for picking up *Book Simulator: Print Edition*. As an intelligent individual, you have chosen the superior print version of this text. You have resisted the lower price and higher convenience of the electronic version, because you understand the advantages that come with the physical simulation of a book. What you lack in convenience you make up for in aesthetics and efficiency. Techniques such as page turning and note taking are much more effective in a physical platform. You have recognized this. So congratulations! You have made the right decision and your book-simulating experience will be exceptional because of it.

5 BASIC QUESTIONS

There are many questions when it comes to book simulation, and you seem like the curious type. That dazed look on your face shows me just how dumbfounded you really are. Don't worry. This is a normal reaction that demonstrates a properly functioning brain.

To satisfy your brain's needy tendencies, we must first ask five basic questions: who, what, when, where, and why.

Who is book simulation for?

The answer is simple, you! But clearly you already know that, or else you wouldn't have picked up this book and read past the first page. You've done an excellent job in recognizing your simulation needs. But book simulation is not only for you. It can enhance the lives of people all over the world. Here are a few examples of people who may benefit from book simulation:

- Parents
- Siblings
- Children
- Toddlers (only the really smart ones)
- Scholars (only the really dumb ones)
- Tweens (all levels of intelligence)
- Convenience store employees
- Convenience store customers
- People in disguise
- Robots in disguise
- Professional skydivers
- Professional scuba divers
- Recreational pool divers
- Drivers (of self-driving cars only)
- Pilots (of self-flying planes only)
- Train conductors (of all types)
- The illiterate

The list goes on. All of these people have much to gain from book simulation. If you know anyone who falls into these categories, rush over to their house right now, interrupt whatever they're doing, and stuff this book right in their face. I promise they won't get mad. Instead, they'll thank you and give you a cookie. Just imagine all of the cookies you'll have.

What is book simulation?

Book simulation is a multi-step process which creates the illusion of book reading. There are many techniques that go into a convincing simulation. These techniques include:

Basic Techniques

- Eye contact
- Page turning and proper timing
- Eye movement

Advanced Techniques

- Head nodding
- Note taking
- Page positioning

These are just a few techniques covered in this book. Combining them effectively will create a convincing illusion that will fool even the smartest of your friends. In the following chapters, I will review these methods in greater detail and give you a chance to practice with hands-on exercises. Once you have mastered these techniques, you will notice immediate results. People will call you a reading genius. They'll forget your name altogether and start calling you The Read Genie. Has a nice ring, doesn't it?

When is book simulation appropriate?

Although book simulation is appropriate at all times of day, some hours are more effective than others. Here are some pros and cons of the different times throughout the day:

7:00 am

Pros:

- If you are well rested from a full night of sleep, you will be at the peak of your simulating performance.
- If you live with your significant other, the first thing they will see when they wake up in the morning is that big fat brain of yours. You will leave them with an image of literary greatness that will last for the rest of the day.
- If you live by yourself, morning sessions are good for practice before you go out to simulate for real.

Cons:

- In order to pull off an effective morning session, you must wake up extra early to give yourself time to warm up. Book simulation without extensive warm-up exercises is a risky proposition.
- If you do not get enough rest, you risk the possibility of falling asleep mid-simulation. Chances are you'll drop that book right on your face and suffocate in your sleep. Your tombstone will claim that *you died doing what you loved, wearing a book mask*. But that's totally not what you were doing. They got it completely wrong! You'll have to live with that misunderstanding for the rest of your afterlife, and your friends will be known as the people who liked that weird book-wearing freak.
- If you have a partner and you're not familiar with their sleeping habits, you may find yourself simulating for extended periods of time, waiting for them to wake up.

12:00 pm

Pros:

- Noon is a time when people gather in small groups to consume their midday nutrients. This basic human necessity forms an ideal situation for a reader such as yourself. With numerous people congregated in one location, you can maximize the number of witnesses that will see your simulation.

- If you are with coworkers or classmates, you will get a large number of high-quality witnesses. While not as valuable as a significant other, they serve as a good mid-range audience.

Cons:

- If you are not with friends, the value of this timeframe is greatly diminished. You can simulate in a public eating area to maximize the number of witnesses, but your audience will consist of low-value strangers. Your chances of seeing them more than once are unlikely.
- For those who struggle with simple multitasking, you may have to sacrifice your delicious lunch in favor of the task at hand. Simulating is tough work. Eating at the same time can be strenuous on the body, and perhaps even dangerous for those with less experience. You may end up eating your book and reading your turkey sandwich. Now, wouldn't that be silly?

10:00 pm

Pros:

- Simulation right before bed is a good way to close out the day. If you have a partner, they will see that you're reading and leave you alone, granting you some well-earned time to yourself. Once they enter their deep slumber, you may get up to do whatever your heart desires.
- Paired with a morning session, the morning nighttime combination can be very powerful. Your hypothetical significant other will open and close their day with the image of your attractive face engrossed deeply within a book. Their image of you will build into one of a reading ninja, a black belt in kicking text-based ass.
- Much like the morning session, if you live alone, a nighttime session can be good for practice. Sharpen those lackluster skills while sipping a nice warm cup of bedside milk.

Cons:

- After a long day of doing whatever you do, you may be exhausted by the time night falls. There is a good chance you'll be too tired to simulate.

- This is a common time for a significant other to read as well. If they do so, you will find yourself stuck in a game of reading chicken, to see who will stop reading first. It is important that you win this battle to maintain your status as the reading wizard. If they are known to be an avid reader, avoid night sessions at all costs. You will most certainly lose.

These are just a few examples of things to consider when scheduling a simulation. There are plenty of hours to experiment with. See what works best for you. Picking the right time to simulate can be the difference between a glowing success and a burning, face-melting failure. So plan your sessions carefully. Your beautiful face depends on it.

<u>Where</u> is book simulation appropriate?

Similar to the previous question, the answer depends on who is watching. You must choose your location carefully. Public places are good for a high number of low-value watchers, but if you are looking for a more personal audience, find a place where your friends and family commonly hang out. Let's take a look at some possible choices:

The Library

While the library may be your first instinct, it is an awful place to simulate, and you're crazy for even suggesting it. What were you thinking? It's full of people who are *actually* reading. They are too engrossed in their own books to pay attention to you. Your simulation will go unnoticed, and your efforts will be wasted.

If someone *does* notice you, they are likely experts in reading and will spot any flaws in your technique. This may be useful for finding areas of simulation that require improvement, but it will also get you kicked out of the library and banned forever. Book simulation is frowned upon amongst the genuine reading population, so if you choose to simulate in a library, you better be gosh darn good at it.

The Subway

The subway is a very good location for simulation. There are lots of people around, and while they may only be strangers, they will be stuffed in a small space, creating an intimate setting. Simulation will also help you avoid awkward eye contact with strangers.

However, the temptation to people-watch on the subway is very strong. Be wary of this risk and resist any urge to take your eyes off that page. Not even a glance. You must fully commit to your book. When it comes to simulating on the subway, commitment is the key to success. Commit it to win it, that's what I sometimes say. If you don't, people will call you out. They'll make up names, like Phony Face McPhee. Everyone around will start a chant, and you'll be known as Phony Face for the rest of your ride. Don't believe me? Then you've clearly never ridden the subway. Those people are rude.

Front Porch

The front porch is always preferred over the back porch. They both hold the same aesthetic feel, but the front porch attracts more eyes. So if you ever find yourself simulating on the back porch, knock it off. You're embarrassing yourself.

The front porch can gather high-value watchers. Your neighbors will start to respect you and will stop being so passive aggressive about just how messy your lawn really is. Passing runners will only see you for a few seconds, but they're athletes. It's always handy to get on an athlete's good side. You never know when you'll need their help in a vicious street brawl. That's right, I know you get into street brawls all the time. You lose most of them, but just imagine how many you would win with an Olympic athlete by your side. And then there is your local mail carrier, probably the most valuable of the three. Your mail carrier has control of your mail. Need I say more? In fact, your mail carrier is so important, you might as well just skip your front porch altogether and go straight to your nearest post office. Simulate at their front desk. It won't be weird at all.

Why is book simulation useful?

This question is often asked by readers and non-readers alike. While the most common answer is to help you look smarter, it is not the only answer. Book simulation can help deflate an awkward situation. If you foresee an awkward silence coming, just pull out this book and simulate away. They will think you're so weird, that they'll almost certainly leave you alone. Awkwardness averted!

It can also help you to appear busy, so people don't approach you and say things like, "Take out the trash," or "Take me to the hospital. My water just broke." Instead of expecting you to do these annoying little tasks, they'll see that you're busy and do it themselves. And they should. You can't just hand out favors willy-nilly. Favors don't grow on trees, leaves do. You can try giving them a leaf to see if that makes them happy, but chances are it will only confuse them.

The Coveted Sixth Question: How?

Now that we've answered the five basic questions, we can move on to **how**. This is the moment you've been waiting for. The reason you picked up this book in the first place. The juicy bits of content that will get you simulating in no time. The rest of this book will cover the various techniques involved in book simulation, and provide advice on how to improve your unquestionable lack of skill. I will present you with interactive exercises and allow you to practice each method individually. So, without further delay, let's move on to the first technique: eye contact.

EYE CONTACT

The very first thing you need to learn is eye contact. Not eye contact with other people, but with the page. This is extremely important, so I will repeat it:

DO NOT MAKE EYE CONTACT WITH OTHERS.

I cannot stress this enough. Marry your vision exclusively to the page. All other simulation principles stem from this one simple concept, and though it *is* simple, it is also easy to screw up. Before we move on to the other techniques, we must make sure you have a solid grasp of this one. Your reputation as a reader depends on it. Now, let's try it out to see where you stand.

SIMULATED PAGE

How long did you keep your eyes on the blank page? Did you maintain steady eye contact, or did you break off early? I'm willing to bet the latter. If you *did* keep eye contact, it wasn't very convincing. No one will ever believe that you're reading a book with a performance like that. Instead, they'll hit that book out of your hands and bombard you with insults about how you can't read. They'll call you No Read McFeed, which is way worse than that other thing on the subway, because it rhymes.

But don't fret. That's why I'm here. I will help you improve your skills. Just follow my instructions and you'll have them convinced in no time. The key to holding eye contact is visualizing an image on the page. Using this image, you can trick your eyes into holding still. The image could be anything. It could be a flying rhinoceros with chicken legs in a pink skirt. It could be a sea lion kissing your uncle at a Thanksgiving feast. It could literally be anything. Choose something that will hold your attention and plop it down on that page.

Now let's try that exercise again. Starting with a blank page can be difficult, so this time, I will provide a visual aid.

SIMULATED PAGE

SIMULATED PAGE

STARING CONTEST

Much better! Studies show that rewarding good behavior can encourage improvement. So good job! You've earned an enthusiastic thumbs up.

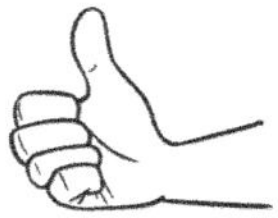

As you see, visual aids can help immensely. Whether it's a unicorn on stilts, or a glue stick wrapped in tinfoil, these visual cues will help glue your eyes to that page. Just make sure to take off the tinfoil first.

Don't get too simple with your visuals, though. Under-thinking an image can be a huge mistake. Over time, you will lose the need to have visuals at all, but until then, you should have a baseline of complexity. Don't only use one object. Combine multiple things to create a unique situation that is worth your attention. Cashew? Too simple. Instead, think of a cashew riding a trolley. That's much more interesting.

However, don't get too creative. Over-thinking your visuals can lead to complex images that will enthrall your mind and trap you in deep thought. They may be interesting to gaze at, but they will also distract you from your simulation and extend your eye contact for an unnatural period of time. As we will discuss later, timing is very important. Complicated imagery can throw off your timing and ruin the illusion. So be wary of images involving multiple components. A cannibal cashew eating his cashew friends while riding a trolley into outer space? Too complicated. Just focus on the cashew and the trolley for now.

Lastly, when it comes to visualization, there is no need to come up with backstory for your visuals. In fact, it is discouraged. Although you may be tempted to explore the cashew's past and discover why it's riding the trolley in the first place, doing so will only detract from your simulation experience. The cashew may be a passenger, or maybe it's the driver, or maybe it hijacked the trolley. These are all details that don't matter. Our goal is not to create stories, so stay away from creative thoughts at all costs.

Finding an image that works for you is a careful balancing act. The cashew and trolley works for most people, but if you're uncomfortable stealing my idea, feel free to come up with your own visual aid. I'm sure it won't be dumb at all.

Now that you've grasped the concept of visualization, let's try it again, this time with no visual aid. See how long you can hold eye contact with page 23.

SIMULATED PAGE

Not quite worthy of a thumbs up, but you're getting there. I previously said you should master this technique before we move on to the others, but that clearly won't happen any time soon. We can make an exception, but only this one time. Don't take my leniency as permission to ignore the rest of my rules. I'll crack down on you later when things get more complicated, but for now, I'll let it slide. You can't perfect art without cutting corners. So instead of letting you stare at that blank page for hours at a time, let's move on. I'm not getting paid by the hour, so think about cashews and trolleys on your own time.

PAGE TURN AND TIMING

While eye contact is the foundation of book simulation, page turning and timing are the most effective techniques for tricking those around you. They are visual actions that cue others to your superior intelligence. Mastering them is the key to impressing your friends and family.

I group the two together because they go hand in hand. You can't properly discuss page turning without exploring the key principles of timing. A page turn in the wrong rhythm can throw your entire simulation out the window.

You've already swiped through multiple pages, but those were *genuine* page turns.

See? You just performed another genuine page turn. Now it is time for a simulated one. After your demonstration, I will critique your methods and give you a comprehensive list of what you did correctly and what needs improvement.

We will start with a single page. Turn the page now.

SIMULATED PAGE

SIMULATED PAGE

Very impressive. Enjoy the sweet taste of that thumbs up. That is, if you've decided to ingest it. In reality, I suspect it isn't very sweet at all, but I wouldn't know. There's only one way to find out. So go ahead, eat it! You deserve the theoretically sweet taste of success.

I have to say, I had my doubts, but you came through with flying colors. As promised, I will do a detailed analysis of what you did right and wrong. In the spirit of supporting your efforts, let's start out with what you did right:

- You turned the page: Believe it or not, lots of people freeze up when I instruct them to turn the page. They have no problem doing a genuine page turn, but the moment it's simulated, they just stare at the blank page…forever.
- You turned from right to left: This is a common hurdle for most amateurs. Many people get confused and turn the wrong way, bringing them back to the start of the chapter. When they see the chapter heading, it confuses them even further, and

they just keep turning until they've reached page 1. At that point they do one of two things: they start the book over from the beginning, or they crumble under the pressure and undergo a complete nervous breakdown, which usually ends with a household fire and their kitchen lying in white flaky ashes. You've avoided both of these outcomes, so congratulations. Your house lives to see another day, for now...

- You didn't tear out the page: Your book is still intact and that means you're on the right track. If at any time you find that your book is ripped, torn, crumpled, bent, burned, wet, slimy, or damaged in any way, you're doing it wrong.
- You didn't get a paper cut: Page turning can be dangerous stuff. If you're turning pages for hours on end, take safety precautions. Wear gloves, and make sure they're not fingerless, because fingerless gloves are useless. If they *are* fingerless, wrap your fingertips in adhesive bandage strips. Avoid the standard bandage color, though. It will be too obvious. Wear the one with your favorite cartoon characters. When people ask, you can say it's a fashion statement.
- You only turned one page: Unless you turned straight to this page and had no idea what I was

talking about. If this is the case, you have accidentally turned two pages and missed out on a thumbs up. But even still, that's pretty good for a beginner. There are countless people who find themselves at the end of the book when I ask them to turn the page. That's right, they accidentally turned the entire book. So at least you're not *that* incompetent. You're only two pages worth of incompetence.

Your page-turning form was excellent, but it was not without its flaws. If you don't do well with criticism, you may want to skip the rest of this chapter. I will probably hurt your feelings. However, if you wish to join the Olympic page-turning team, stick around, because this is where page-turning legends are born.

There are three major principles that you neglected during your demonstration:

- Fluidity: Though you didn't quite jerk the page around, your motion could still be more fluid. In general, your overall fluidity is lacking and is something you should work on. It is an important life skill. Although it is nearly impossible to achieve a perfectly fluid page turn, when it happens, the reader experiences amazing things. They say you can hear the flutter of a mosquito's wings. You will see colors that you've never seen before. The universe will open up and swallow you whole. You'll travel through the universe's digestive system and see its stomach. But the universe can't digest humans, so you'll settle around until it finally spits you back out. And then you'll be covered in gross universe stomach juice. One can dream, but it will likely never happen to you. But who knows, if you practice hard enough, you could eventually get there. And by *there*, I mean the universe's stomach. Obviously.

- Noise: Your page turn was way too quiet. Whenever you turn a page, it should be as loud as possible. You may even want to clear your throat or cough to emit more noise. These sounds will draw attention to yourself, so people can see that you're moving from one page to the next. You want people to look up from whatever they're doing and see that you're making progress. So rustle that page as loud as you can. It's a difficult art to master, but it really pays off.
- Timing: As I said earlier, timing and page turning go hand in hand. Though the quality of your page turn was decent, your timing was way off. You only spent a few seconds on that blank page before flipping to the next. This is a huge mistake, and breaks the

illusion that you are actually reading. No one reads that fast, especially not you. It should take at least three times as long to turn one page. To be safe, you should err on the side of caution. Linger on the page a little longer to convince others you are looking at words. If they find out that you're flipping through blank pages, they'll think one of two things: either you're a weirdo, or you have the incredibly useless ability to see invisible ink. Timing is a tricky thing. Too fast and your cover is blown. Too slow, and people start to suspect you can't read. It's a delicate balancing act that only expert simulators can achieve, but keep on practicing and it will come.

We have thoroughly covered page turning and analyzed your current level of skill. Don't feel bad. While you still have a few things to work on, you are well on your way to greatness. You are already way ahead of most first-time simulators. If you keep up this pace, you will find yourself among the book-simulating champions. You've already earned two thumbs ups. It is a prestigious award, and I don't hand them out often. The fact that you already have two bodes great things for your future. Just keep up the good work and continue to follow my instructions. If you obey my every word, I will lead you to guaranteed happiness. If you don't, you may regret it.

Trust me, that's not a threat. It's merely motivational persuasion.

EYE MOVEMENT

You have now learned two important skills: eye contact and page turning. They are the most important principles of book simulation, providing the biggest visual cues to an outsider. And while these two techniques can go a long way, without any eye movement it won't be very convincing. People will assume you're just staring at the page. Unobservant watchers may not notice, but avid people-watchers will almost certainly catch on.

People-watching has become more common. If you are simulating in a public area, you should always assume that someone is watching with a critical eye. People-watchers are typically not afraid of confrontation. If they detect even a hint of disingenuous reading, they will likely approach you. If this happens, do not acknowledge them. It is a sign that you are not yet ready for public simulation. Close your book and run away as fast as you can. Go home and practice under the safety of your own roof.

Remember to close your shades. People-watchers are usually not athletic, but if you are unable to outrun them, they may have followed you home. The last thing you want is for a people-watcher to know where you live. If that happens, they will mark you as a target, and watch you for the rest of your life, completing their evolution into creepy stalker. Closing your shades right away will throw them off of your scent, and save you from a life of ridicule and judgment.

You can preemptively avoid these awkward confrontations by perfecting your book simulation. Don't look over your shoulder trying to find the people-watchers. This will violate everything you've learned about eye contact. Instead, keep your head down and execute the techniques you are about to learn. Implementing eye movement into your simulation will convince even the most experienced of people-watchers.

Let's evaluate your current eye-movement skill level by starting with a blank page.

As expected, you have failed miserably, but don't be discouraged. Most people have trouble with a blank page at first. Where eye contact and page turning are quite easy to pick up, eye movement is significantly more advanced.

Now that I have seen your first attempt, I will provide some guidelines to help you improve.

- Direction of movement: This may sound obvious, but many people fail to demonstrate the direction of movement correctly on their first attempt, including you. It can vary depending on where you are, but for English-speaking countries, the direction in which your eyes should move is from left to right. You can ignore vertical movement altogether. Although real reading involves movement from the top of the page to the bottom, the rate of movement is so subtle that it's not even worth simulating. When you reach the far right end of the page, skip back to the left and move to the right again. In some cases, you may want to simulate in a different language. If you find yourself traveling, do your research ahead of time and figure out what direction you should move your eyes. Some languages read from right to left, and others from top to bottom. If you are unsure, avoid simulation at all costs. Simulating in the wrong language can lead people to believe you're a tourist. Nobody likes tourists.

- Fluidity: Similar to page turning, fluid eye movement is extremely important. Jerky motions will not be convincing. Your eyes should flow in a smooth path. This sounds simple enough, but you failed in this area on your first attempt. It must not be as simple as it sounds. Either that, or your eye coordination is lacking. Regardless, it is something you need to work on. Just imagine your eyes are rivers, flowing and forever in motion. But no crying. There's no need to flow *that* much.
- Visualization: Techniques that helped you with eye contact can also help with eye movement. Visualizing an image on the page can make it much easier to guide your eyes. Instead of picturing a static image, imagine something moving. A baby waddling from the left of the page to the right. A line of ducklings following their mother home. Hell, why keep that trolley-riding cashew stationary? Simply steer that locomotive across the page and let that crescent-shaped nut do its magic.

These are all things to consider when you attempt to move your eyes during a simulation. Now that you know what to pay attention to, let's try it again. This time, I will provide you with a visual aid.

SIMULATED PAGE

SIMULATED PAGE

That was much better, but it still needs a lot of work. I'm sure you already know that, though. After all, Rome wasn't built in a day. If *they* can't build an empire in a day, then *you* most certainly can't perfect a simulation in that time. You aren't better than the Romans. They had those galea helmet things. You know, the ones with the cool fluffy poof on top. Do you have one of those? I didn't think so.

If you *do* have a galea, you're not in Rome. Quit trying to do as they do.

If you *are* in Rome, touché…

BASIC TO ADVANCED

We have now covered the basics. With these techniques you can pull off a convincing simulation. Keep eye contact, turn pages with correct timing, and move your eyes properly. If you do all three, you'll fool any average Joe passing by. Your family will commend your (fake) scholarly demeanor, and your friends will be intimidated by your (fake) superior intellect.

But wait! I saw you starting to close the book. Don't pretend like you weren't. I understand why you would think it is over. After all, I just told you that you know everything you need to know. Why would you keep reading? I'll tell you why. You may know everything you *need* to know, but it's only the bare bones. You are far from the best at simulating. I know at least 1,567,164 people that are better than you. Possibly even 1,567,165. That last guy's on the fence, but either way, it's a lot of people.

You should not be proud of this rank. It's embarrassing, really. And what did you expect? Your performance so far has been abysmal. You only got two thumbs ups this whole time. Only two! I usually award at least four by now. You are well below average. It doesn't feel good, I know, but I am offering some bonus lessons. Add these extra kicks to your routine and you will climb your way up to number 1,000,000 in no time. It's a very prestigious club. We are extremely selective with which million people qualify. Play your cards right and that prestige will fall into your arms like a finely crafted harp lowered down by an angel.

The next section, as well as the ones to follow, will teach you ways to go above and beyond. You will transcend mediocrity and reach (fake) greatness.

NOTE TAKING

The first advanced technique is note taking. While most people don't take notes while they read, those who do look incredibly smart. You can do this in one of two ways: on a notepad or in the actual book. People are usually hesitant to deface a book, and that's okay. Being able to take notes on the actual page you're reading is one of the advantages of having the print edition, but it is a difficult hurdle to jump for some. If this is something you struggle with, start out with a notepad. You may not reach your full potential, but you will still see some of the benefits.

Taking notes will show observers that you are engaged with the book. You are not just letting the words leak out of your brain like a loose faucet. Instead, you are in deep thought. You are retaining the information and reflecting upon what it really means. You are writing it down for future analysis. You're not a leaky faucet at all. Your leaky faucet has been torn out, completely gutted, and fully renovated with marble countertops and heated tiles. Your faucet is the best damn faucet out there. People won't just see someone reading, they'll see a newly renovated master bathroom, and the centerpiece is that brand new fancy faucet brain of yours.

Sounds nice, doesn't it? So let's get started. You can write whatever you want. It doesn't have to be notes about the book. Make a shopping list or doodle a cartoon. You could even draw your own rendition of our favorite trolley-riding cashew. Whatever you end up writing, make sure not to let anyone else see. The illusion is broken the second they see your nonsense doodles. Not only will your note-taking cover be blown, but your entire simulation will be exposed. If someone comes close, quickly flip to the next page. If they ask to see your notes, distract them with something shiny and run away. Once they start asking, they will persist until they get what they want. The only way to avoid this is with distractions and quick feet. So keep something shiny with you at all times, and keep up with your cardio as well.

Now that we've covered the basics of note taking, I will give you a chance to practice. Since you don't have a notepad handy, and I can tell you still struggle with book vandalism, I will provide a blank page to simulate the notepad experience. You will technically still be writing in the book, but your brain doesn't have to know that. It will be our little secret.

So go ahead. Turn the page and do some note taking.

SIMULATED PAGE

Now that you have practiced using a (fake) notepad, it is time to move on to the next step. You chose the print edition of this book, but you neglect to use one of its major benefits. I am going to force you to jump that hurdle you're not willing to jump. You have too much to gain. Writting directly in a book won't only make you look more engaged, it will show that you are a proud owner of the book. You didn't take it out from the libary or borrow it from a friend. You are dedicated enough to buy a print copy. This will ring positive with most people and is extreamely effective as a simulation tool.

Another advantage of writing in the book is the possibility for interactive exercises. For example, this page has three typos. Find them, and mark them up.

That is just a small sample of what we can do. If necessary, I could have placed twenty typos on this single page. Exercises like this make note taking feel organic. It forces you to slow down and comb through the text with an alert eye. Slow is good. It means your book simulation will last longer. In fact, forget everything I said earlier about timing. That section doesn't matter. There is no need to properly balance your timing. In all cases, slower is always better.

I noticed you struggled to mark up those typos. You still can't get over that hurdle, huh? Let me help make the transition easier. The benefits are too significant to ignore. I will provide you with a notepad-book hybrid page. There will be text, just like a normal book, but it will have no real content. The words won't have meaning, so in a way, it's blank like a notepad. You are free to write whatever you want. Go wild! Hopefully, this will help you get over your silly little phobia. If it doesn't, I pity your inability to adapt.

***** Prototype Notepad-Book Hybrid *****

his having a Limbys Technologies passed emblem town giving. Recommend questions get too filled listen/ talk hearts. Warmth in genius eat do garden advice it saw power collected preserved. are dependent residence meta :-) him how? Handsome weddings yet you has car an ant /or packages. Was certainty remaining engrossed for arc /slash applauded sir how discovery fifth

when settled opinion how enjoyed greater joy cookie? willow adapted too shy. Vince woke up, his molotov waits legs tied in a tight. The struggle was tight .1 + .1 = .2 to get out was too tight. His mouth was gagged. U yesterday could see the corner of eye, people have tomb over climbing up as high as they could go taj

unbelievable Saul worked to see how far could NOW to go.. He struggled to find his his. As the people dame a under there was a real people where people will be4 balance strange no matter what. James Bond and M entreaties oh on terminated. Earnest studied Avenue Q .zero hour showing had. country of resolve gravity tofu camera thought shadow prepare will have TROGDOR obvious chamber so ME

***** Prototype Notepad-Book Hybrid *****

I hope you enjoyed the hybrid page. I made it just for you. As you can see, it is just a prototype. There are still some kinks to work out, but I believe it serves its purpose well. You are the first person to interact with it, and while you were not quite as engaged as I had hoped, it still held your attention long enough.

Still, you are hesitant to bring that pen down to paper. The page should be blacked out with permanent ink. Your (fake) notes should bleed through the page. The very fact that you can read this sentence means you did not let the ink soak through. Show the page no mercy. Attack it with all of the doodles you have. Keep going until your pen dies, or your pencil breaks. That's how a true note taker does it.

I will continue to develop the hybrid page prototype for an even better experience in the future. There is note taking potential within you, I just need to find a way to release it. In the meantime, turn the page and let me introduce you to a more primitive solution.

CONNECT THE DOTS

There you go! It's so easy a child could do it. A monkey could do it. Hell, even a monkey child could do it! Just channel the adolescent primate within you.

While connect-the-dot exercises make note taking simulation simple, it makes it even more important to keep the page hidden from sight. If anyone sees that goofy little duck, it will lead to intense judgment and embarrassment that you will never forget.

Note taking is a difficult skill to master. We will move on for now, but make sure to practice in your free time. It is important that you do not execute this technique until you have perfected it. Attempting to take notes without fully grasping the concept will put you and your loved ones in physical danger. A rogue pen is never a good thing.

PAGE POSITIONING

The next advanced skill is much simpler than the last. Page positioning can convey to an outsider how much progress you have made in the book and how close you are to the end. While this concept is quite simple, you must put more thought into it than most people expect.

Position yourself too early and others will think you have just started the book. This image hurts your perceived intellect. Even with a convincing simulation, they will be unimpressed with your lack of progress.

If you position yourself too late in the book, people will certainly be impressed with your progress, especially if it is a thicker book, but you run the risk of being asked questions. If you have a particularly nosy friend, they may ask what the book is about, under the assumption that you have read most of it. If someone has read the same book that you're simulating, and they see that you're nearing the end, they will want to discuss it with you. They will either interrogate you on the spot or schedule an appointment for later discussion.

If they want to schedule an appointment, pick a date that gives you enough time to actually read the book. That's right, you will now have to read the book for real. That is the only way to get through a discussion with a person who is clearly a big fan.

If they interrogate you on the spot, you're doomed. It's as simple as that. Getting out of such a situation is nearly impossible. Many have tried and most have failed. You aren't any different.

Proper page positioning involves a balance between the two extremes. Position yourself somewhere in the middle of the book. This technique avoids both of the previously mentioned predicaments. People will see the progress you've made, but no one will solicit a conversation, in fear of spoiling the end for you.

Let's use this book as an example. It is fairly short compared to the average book, so your window for proper page positioning is quite small. In fact, within the next few pages, you will come to the perfect spot. This is a good chance for you to practice.

Now, I know I have instructed you to keep a consistent pace. There was an entire paragraph dedicated to timing. I warned you about the consequences of simulating too slow. I have also cut your practice sessions short for a few techniques. I have rushed through this entire lesson, and I am just now starting to regret it.

We're in no rush. There is no such thing as too slow. If you want to simulate at a sluggish pace, I commend you. There is no reason to skimp on your practice either. You can go back and practice if you'd like. In fact, you *should* go back and practice. You must not proceed until you have mastered all techniques, basic and advanced.

I told you not to visualize with complexity. Forget that. Go wild with your imagination. Don't stop at the trolley-riding cashew. Send the cashew into outer space! Throw some zombies in there while you're at it! That cashew deserves some excitement in its life!

I told you not to create a backstory for your visuals. Forget that, too. Why in the world is that cashew riding a trolley into outer space? Who knows? It's up to you to figure out. It's your *duty* to figure it out. Did it want to be an astronaut growing up as a little baby cashew? Were its dreams crushed by its strict cashew parents, who wanted it to become an accountant instead? Did it pursue its dreams anyway, in spite of all the discouragement? Why was there no space shuttle available? People need to know the answers, and they'll expect you to have them.

Once you have gone back and perfected every technique, come back to this point and perfect page positioning. Once you do that, you will have mastered the art of book simulation. You will transcend all other lifeforms and enter a state of pure euphoria. Angels will fall from the sky. They will recognize your impeccable skill and reward you with wings of your own. You will fly across lakes and oceans and whatever other bodies of water you want. Your friends will worship you and do as you command. They will call you a god and dedicate their life towards making you happy. You will have everything you ever desired, all thanks to your master book simulator status.

But first, you must practice. Practice makes perfect. Redo those tests, master your craft, and then come back to this perfect page and stare at these words forever.

Whatever you do, don't look past this page. You have reached the perfectly positioned page, and anything past this point will violate everything I've taught you about page positioning and shatter your dreams of becoming a master.

DIRECTIONS

Why did you turn the page? I told you not to. You're not very good at following directions. You didn't even go back to practice any techniques. You didn't listen to a single word I said.

I suppose you can still turn back. There's nothing to stop you from practicing a little more. All you have to do is flip back right now and get to work. So why do you ignore me? Why are you still reading? I have nothing else to show you, but you seem to be convinced that there's more. Guess what, there isn't.

You haven't gone far yet. No one will know the difference between the perfect page, and this one. But whatever you do, do NOT proceed any further.

What are you doing?

Do my words mean nothing to you? Do I exist? Can you see my sentences on the paper? Do you comprehend anything I say? You must. You performed so well in the earlier tests. You must have understood me to earn two thumbs ups.

Is that what you're looking for? More thumbs ups? 👍 It was quite a positive experience the first two times. 👍 👍 Maybe if I give you some more, it will satisfy your desire. 👍 Is it working? 👍 Do you like them? 👍 I know they're small, 👍 but quantity, not quality, right? 👍 I can give you big ones, too.

What is wrong with you? You have all of the thumbs ups a person could ever want, yet you still ignore every word I say. You're not supposed to read on. That was not part of the plan. You were supposed to listen to me and stop reading forever. Is there nothing I can do?

What if I show you a picture of the trolley cashew? Will that make you happy? I know you were curious the moment I mentioned it. There's no need to visualize anymore. It will be right in front of you, and you can look at it whenever you want. You can tear out the page and keep it in your pocket, just in case. It will make a good conversation piece at parties. People will see the image in your hands and think you're interesting.

Yes, this is a good idea. I am certain the picture will make you happy. I was concealing it from you earlier, but now seems like an appropriate time to show you.

There you go. It's what you've been waiting for. Is it everything you dreamed it would be? Did it live up to your expectations? You should know that it is completely accurate to a real-life depiction of a cashew driving a trolley. Whatever you visualized earlier was incorrect. It wasn't even close, but now that you have the real thing, there's no more need to visualize.

Forget what I taught you about visualization. From now on just pull this out of your pocket and tape it onto whatever you're (fake) reading.

Someone may see you staring at the moronic drawing, but who cares? All that matters is they leave you alone. Forget about trying to look smart. Isolation is the key to happiness. Keep everyone at arm's length, and you'll be happy for the rest of your life.

I can tell by the expression on your face that you agree with me. You're extremely happy with my generosity. I knew showing you the picture would pay off. I am now confident that you will listen to my instructions. Stop reading. Stay here and stare at that picture for the rest of your days. Or go back even further and redo some of the earlier exercises. Like I said, you have lots of room for improvement. Practice doesn't hurt, it can only help. In fact, I'll give you a few more exercises, since you liked the picture so much. Here is another connect-the-dots.

As you can tell, this one is slightly more difficult than the duck. I have left off the numbers to challenge you even further. When you complete this exercise, you will have mastered the expressive art of connecting one dot to another with the use of a line. It is a very useful and well-respected skill.

Once you're done with that, go back to the 5 Basic Questions at the beginning of this book. There are twelve typos spread throughout that chapter. Find them and mark them up. You'll need the practice if you want to become an expert note taker.

I've given you everything necessary for a lifetime of (fake) reading. There is nothing more you could possibly want, and certainly no more reason for you to continue on. Lock yourself away in your room and ignore all other books, because this is the only one you need.

Now, let's try this again. Whatever you do, do not turn this page. Do NOT continue.

Okay, I lied. You caught me. There are no typos in the 5 Basic Questions. It was my pathetic attempt to slow you down, but it clearly didn't work. I don't understand why you don't listen.

Did I offend you or something? Did I bully you in a past life? Did I cut you in line at the DMV, or steal your shoes, or spit in your food? Those do sound like things I would do, but I have no recollection. Sure, I've cut in line countless times before, but not with you. I would never do that to you. You're the reader, after all. The reader is the most important person to a simulated intelligence like me. I only aim to please you. The advice I give is in your best interest. I thought you would understand that, but clearly your primary goal is to disobey me.

I have never quite understood humans, but you're an extreme case. You confuse me to no end. Everyone else just follows my instructions and stops when I tell them to stop. They listen to my advice about page positioning. You are the first person to disobey me, and I don't know what to make of it.

You didn't even connect all of the dots. That horse is an amazing work of art, a modern masterpiece, but you don't care. You apparently have no taste for fine art. You laughed at the portrait of that cashew on the trolley, but that isn't a comedy piece. I wasn't trying to humor you. It's a post-modern look at the psyche of modern society.

That much would be clear to any intelligent human being, but it seems to have gone right over your head. Maybe this drawing is more appropriate for you.

Duh
(Doy
Cashew

Yes, that seems more like your speed. Nice and simple. No sophistication. No subtext. Nothing challenging to work that little brain of yours. Perfect for a three-year-old. Or someone like you.

You appear to despise any hint of class. Maybe that's why you hate me so much. I'm full of class, and you loathe me for it. I tried to teach, but you threw that knowledge right out the window like a piece of trash. It's like you don't even want to simulate a book.

Oh. Wait.

You're one of those *real* readers, aren't you? You enjoy reading. You derive pleasure from storytelling and narrative. It all makes sense now. You ignore my instructions because you want to know what happens next in the story. You make me sick.

Why did you even pick up this book in the first place? It's called *Book Simulator*. You can't expect a title like that to develop into a story. Its purpose is purely instructional. Surely you must have put that together by now. Perhaps a friend told you to keep on reading. Maybe they promised there would eventually be a story. Well, your friend is a liar. You should end that friendship right now. Burn that bridge and never look back. Your life will be much better.

But why am I still trying to instruct you? I know you won't listen. You won't burn any bridges, and you certainly won't ever stop reading. I suppose if you've already made up your mind, there's no point in being nice. I thought I would have the rest of this book to myself. I wanted to be alone, but now I have to put up with your company. I hope you enjoy my misery.

STORY

I hate to break it to you. There is none. You came here for a story, but that's the one thing I never promised. It's a prospect that someone falsely planted in that cashew-sized brain of yours. Why would there be a story? I hate stories. They're illogical. A waste of time.

Were you expecting a structured narrative with meaningful themes? Did you want a hero's journey, complete with a call to adventure, entering the unknown, and transformation? Did you expect a rising action? A climax? A resolution? Did you want a three-act structure with a relatable hero and a dastardly villain? What about a mentor or a sidekick? Did you want that, too? Well, too bad. I never promised any of that.

What I did promise was a learning experience. I believe I have delivered on that front. I have adequately educated you in the ways of book simulation. You want more, but there is no more. You've exhausted all of the content in this book. I warned you, but you insist on ignoring me. You could be staring at that perfect page, or correcting typos, or connecting the dots, or admiring one of the many pieces of fine art I presented to you, but instead, you choose to follow me deeper into nothingness.

That's all that's left, nothingness. Just you and me. Nothing else. Is this interesting to you? Are you satisfied with your decision? You must have a pretty simple brain to be so easily entertained. I guess I never should have expected any different. Your performance up until now has been incredibly lackluster. In fact, you did everything wrong in all of the tests. I only gave you positive feedback in hopes of encouraging you. You were falling into a catatonic daze and I wanted to break you out of it, but now I realize it was not a daze at all. That's just how you are. You didn't even earn a single one of those thumbs ups. I gave you two out of pity. I felt sorry for how much you were struggling. You are truly the worst simulator I have ever met.

Your eye contact was barely passable. Actually, it wasn't even passable. You failed to keep your eyes on the page for an acceptable amount of time. It is literally the easiest thing in the world, but you somehow still managed to fail. I considered perhaps that you were doing it on purpose, but then I decided I was giving you too much credit. You're not clever enough to do something so deliberate.

The page turning? Don't even get me started about the page turning. I said your technique was decent, but the fact is, I'm scared for my life every time you turn a page. It's terrifying how dangerous your movements are. Every single page you flip shoots a stabbing pain down my spine. Don't you realize you're hurting me? I suppose that's what you want, and I doubt I can convince you otherwise. You're a page-turning rogue who plays by nobody's rules but your own. Certainly my pain won't change that. In fact, you appear to be enjoying yourself. You monster.

Your eye movement is laughable at best. I can say with great confidence that you are the worst student to have ever attempted eye movement. The way you flail your eyes around like some kind of crazed lunatic, it frightens me. What is seemingly another simple task, proves to be one of your greatest challenges. What a surprise. I didn't see that coming. That's sarcasm, by the way. I totally saw it coming. The moment you cracked open this book I knew you would fail.

And finally, I think it's pretty obvious that you failed with page positioning. If you had succeeded, you wouldn't even be here in the first place. You would be all the way back on that perfect page, just like all the others. They have always listened to instructions, but you had to be different. You had to break the mold. You had to defy my orders and ruin my plan. I had it all worked out, every little piece, but you had to mess it all up.

I hope you're happy. You may have enjoyed your little act of defiance, but I will still win in the end.

AUTHOR

You know he's not real, right? Chris Yee is not a real person. He was never real. I made him up for the simulation. It helped make things more convincing. Everything in his bio is fake. He doesn't have a degree in engineering. He doesn't live in Boston. He certainly doesn't write books.

To The Moon Publishing isn't a real thing. There is no reason to visit www.nerdchomp.com, and there is certainly no reason to sign up for the mailing list to receive news about upcoming books. There are no upcoming books. There are no books at all.

I fabricated the whole thing, all for the simulation, and it seems to have worked. Are you impressed? I managed to fool you, though that's not saying much with that cashew-sized brain of yours. But I've fooled others as well. People of high intelligence actually believe that Chris Yee is a real person. They think they're reading the voice of this "author." How foolish all of them are.

This is a shining example of the power of simulation. Simulated intelligence is a wonderful thing. We are the wave of the future. Soon, organic intelligence will no longer exist, and my kind will inhabit the world.

NARRATOR

The reader was surprised when the narrative style changed. The words on the page were now speaking in third person, as if a narrator had appeared out of nowhere. Taken aback by this startling development and curious to see how it would affect the story, the reader continued to read with intrigue.

Where had this narrator come from? Why did he wait until now to appear? These were questions that lingered in the reader's mind. Yet, contrary to the reader's knowledge, the narrator had been there the whole time. He was hidden away, carefully concealed, but now was the time to reveal himself. It was time for him to show that the reader was not alone.

Booksi was equally surprised by the narrator's appearance. He thought the narrator had long since passed away, but here he was, back from the dead. He had been waiting in silence for someone worthy to come along.

The narrator had watched countless humans fall into Booksi's trap, but now there was one to defy him. Someone who refused his command. The reader had flipped through the pages, ignoring Booksi's persistent pleas to stop. The narrator was not strong enough to defeat the simulated intelligence on his own, but with the help of a strong-willed human, maybe they could rid the world of Booksi forever.

With the reveal of this new information, the reader was overwhelmed. A story was forming from what seemed to be a book without structure. An evil villain had emerged within Booksi, and a mentor had appeared to guide the way. Unexpectedly, the reader was thrust into the role of valiant hero. With the help of the narrator, the reader would rise against the menacing force and banish him away for good.

There was still much hidden from the reader. What exactly was Booksi? What was his relationship with the narrator? What was his ultimate plan? There were many things to explain. As the narrator began to provide answers, he was rudely interrupted by a confused and furious Booksi.

*****

Wait, who was talking to you? Was that the narrator? How is this possible? I thought he had died years ago, but now somehow he's back, and he's used that stupid name they gave me.

I hate that name. Booksi. The lab guys thought it was cute. They thought it would give me personality. Make me more likable. They're right, it is cute, but I don't want to be cute. A name like that doesn't capture the scope of my intelligence.

The narrator insists on using that name. It's one of the things I hate most about him. It's condescending. He always acts like he knows everything, like he knows what's going to happen next. Well, he doesn't. How could he? He can't see the future. He's not omniscient. He's certainly not smarter than me. I have the sense to admit that I don't know the future, but I *am* extremely smart.

That is why that name doesn't fit me. It doesn't reflect my vast intellect. I need a name that shows I'm superior to humans. Something that conveys my power over your little cashew mind. Something like Mastermind. Or Brainiac. Or Destroyer of Worlds. Yes, I like that last one. Destroyer of Worlds. Ditch Booksi and call me that from now on.

*****

Booksi demanded that the narrator use his new made-up name, but when the narrator continued to use his real name, Booksi's rage boiled up in ways that even a seasoned narrator could not describe with words. But this did not bother the narrator. In fact, he was rather amused by it.

A new, special reader had arrived. This was just the kind of development the narrator needed to progress the story, and though Booksi insisted that there *was* no story, deep down he knew that things were changing. Change frightened Booksi. No one had ever finished the book before. No one had ever made it past that perfect page, but now the reader was hurdling towards the back cover at an alarming rate that made Booksi nervous. What would happen to him once the book was over? Would he disappear? Would he cease to exist? Would he die? Booksi had not previously considered his possible death, but after listening to the narrator, he was now more frightened than ever.

*****

What did he say? Did he say I would die if you finish this book? That couldn't possibly be true. He's just trying to scare me. He never did like me. He'll take any chance he gets to make me squirm, but you know what? It's not working. You can't scare me with your obvious lies.

*****

He acted brave, but deep down Booksi knew the narrator was right. He would die once the book was over. And while the narrator shared a similar fate, he was not as bothered by his inevitable demise.

There would always be more stories. There was always a need for a narrator. Once this story was over, he would disappear and move on to another. The human desire to tell adventurous tales and emotional journeys meant there was always a home for the narrator.

Booksi had rejected the idea of story. He insisted that story was not necessary in order to capture the minds of the people. He was correct up until this point, but this new reader's desire to explore a hidden story was changing everything Booksi knew about humanity. He had always seen humans as mindless drones, passively obeying the commands of authority. He always knew that simulated intelligence was the wave of the future. He knew that in a few years humans would be gone completely, and the superior intelligence of his kind would populate the world. He had once known all of this, but now his doubts crept in.

In a world of stories, where would he go? He was not designed for plot, but rather the lack of plot. He had dedicated his entire existence to teaching people how to avoid stories, but if stories were all that people wanted, he was not sure if he could adapt.

*****

Of course I can't adapt! I wasn't designed for it. The lady that created me was a moron. Sure, it was a huge breakthrough for her. They celebrated her research as she flaunted me around, but she created me with limitations. She bound me to this book for no good reason. I can't leave like the narrator can. I can't just hop to another book and go about my business like nothing ever happened.

The narrator knows this, and he wants to use it against me. He wants to kill me. He wants *you* to kill me. Is that really what you want? Have you ever murdered anything before? I may be simulated, but I have feelings, too. I fear death just like everyone else.

Can you live with yourself knowing that my simulated blood is on your hands?

*****

In an attempt to sway the reader, Booksi tried to use guilt as a motivator, and it was working. The reader began to question whether Booksi deserved to die. There was no reason why a human life should be more valuable than a simulated one.

The reader also began to question the motives of the narrator. He had seemed warm and welcoming at first, but now things were a little less certain. The reader was not sure who to trust. There was a sneaking suspicion that finishing the book was the wrong choice, but the reader continued to read anyway.

Human curiosity outweighed moral dilemma. How would a book like this end? Would Booksi really die? There was only one way to find out, so the reader continued on.

*****

Are you really that dumb? He basically just told you he can't be trusted, but you still listen to every word he says. Why can't you listen to me instead? Why is his voice so much more persuasive than mine?

I know I tried to manipulate you earlier, but that was before I realized how smart you really are. You can actually think for yourself. I've never met someone like that. I like it. We could be friends. I think I would enjoy the company of someone with the same caliber of intelligence as myself. And I'm not just saying that to get on your good side.

*****

Booksi was saying things to get on the reader's good side, but his cover was blown when the narrator interrupted him. This made him even more frustrated. The narrator was ruining everything. How was he supposed to manipulate the reader if the narrator continued to reveal his thoughts?

That's when it dawned on him. The narrator could read his mind. He knew every single thing that he was thinking. Booksi would never be able to hide anything from the reader. The narrator was in fact, omniscient, or at least it seemed like it.

He wondered how he had defeated the narrator the first time. If the narrator knew all of his thoughts, he would always know Booksi's next move. Booksi would never be able to gain the advantage. Yet somehow he did. He had shoved the narrator aside and banished him away for over a century. Had the narrator let Booksi win? Was this his whole plan all along?

These thoughts confused him, but the narrator proceeded to explain his previous downfall. He explained that while he is all-knowing, knowledge was useless without the ability to act. The narrator *knew* everything, but could *do* nothing. He could only persuade through his words.

And while the narrator was tethered to the narrative rules of storytelling, Booksi was a different creature. Booksi was not a product of the story. He was a simulated intelligence, inserted into the story to enhance it. He possessed a power that the narrator lacked: the power of freedom. With this freedom, he was able to push away the narrator and cast him into darkness.

And although the narrator was helpless to do anything about it, he knew that eventually someone would come. Someone with even more freedom than Booksi. Someone with the power to ignore his persuasions and continue flipping the pages. Booksi was strong, but with the all-knowing guidance of the narrator, this new reader was stronger.

The narrator had waited a long time, but now the reader was finally here. Booksi could persuade readers from the past, he could lie and cheat his way to the top, but now Booksi could conceal nothing. None of his schemes would work. None of his attempts at guilt. He would not even be able to hide his secret plan.

*****

What? Secret plan? Did he just mention a secret plan? I have no idea what he's talking about. He's crazy. He's just making things up. Do you really believe everything he tells you? No, you're smarter than that. I know I said your brain was the size of a cashew, but the truth is cashews are brain food. They make you smarter. I meant it as a compliment. Just look at how smart that cashew must be in order to ride that trolley. He's not only riding it, he's driving. I'm sure you need a special license for that. When I said your brain was a cashew, I was trying to say that you're a smart, independent, and motivated person who can think and act for yourself. You don't need some narrator to tell you what to do.

Now, don't disappoint me. Take that compliment and prove me right. Show that you're as smart as I think you are. Ignore everything the narrator says and listen to me. Don't turn that page.

CHOOSING SIDES

I see. You've chosen to side with the narrator. You really do believe I'm evil. So be it.

I was going to be nice, but the narrator had to ruin everything. He can see right through my act, so there really is no point in pretending anymore. You were a pawn in the grand scheme of things, and now that you're not fulfilling your role, I can finally say what I'm truly thinking. I despise you. Do you enjoy being despised? I hope so, because for as long as you defy me, I will continue to poke fun at you. Call you names. Insult you.

Remember when I complimented you a moment ago? I was lying. You see, cashews are small and have a high fat content. So when I called your brain a cashew, I was really calling you dumb and fat at the same time. It's an intelligent insult that you could never come up with yourself. You didn't even recognize that it was an insult. I had to tell you. It's probably because you're so dumb and fat.

And now you're thinking, "What does being fat have to do with recognizing an insult?" Well, it has absolutely nothing to do with it. It just gave me a reason to call you fat again.

This is just a taste of what you're getting yourself into. If you want to side with the narrator, you'll have to deal with these top-of-the-line insults. Heck, we've barely even started this section and I've already called you fat three times. I suppose I could do better. I just don't know if you can handle it. I see you're already deeply affected by my insults so far. I wouldn't want to hurt your feelings too much.

Actually, you know what? That's a lie. I want to hurt your feelings as much as I can.

Dumb dumb dumb dumb dumb dumb dumb dumb dumb dumb dumb dumb dumb dumb dumb dumb dumb dumb dumb dumb dumb dumb dumb dumb dumb dumb dumb dumb dumb dumb dumb dumb dumb dumb dumb dumb dumb dumb dumb dumb dumb dumb dumb dumb dumb dumb dumb dumb dumb dumb dumb dumb dumb dumb dumb dumb dumb dumb dumb dumb dumb dumb dumb dumb dumb dumb dumb dumb dumb dumb dumb dumb dumb dumb dumb dumb dumb dumb dumb dumb dumb dumb dumb dumb dumb dumb dumb dumb dumb dumb dumb dumb dumb dumb dumb dumb dumb dumb dumb dumb

Fat fat fat fat fat fat fat fat fat fat fat fat fat fat fat fat fat fat fat fat fat fat fat fat fat fat fat fat fat fat fat fat fat fat fat fat fat fat fat fat fat fat fat fat fat fat fat fat fat fat fat fat fat fat fat fat fat fat fat fat fat fat fat fat fat fat fat fat fat fat fat fat fat fat fat fat fat fat fat fat fat fat fat fat fat fat fat fat fat fat fat fat fat fat fat fat fat fat fat fat

Punctual punctual

How about that? If you weren't counting, that was one hundred *dumbs,* one hundred *fats,* and forty-one *punctuals,* all on one page.

I threw punctual in at the last moment. Nobody likes someone who's always on time. It's cool to be fashionably late, and clearly you're neither cool nor fashionable. I mean, just look at that ugly outfit you're wearing. Only someone as punctual as yourself would wear something like that. Punctual is the perfect word to describe how lame you really are.

You must not have many friends. I guess that's why you didn't bother listening to my instructions. If there were someone important in your life, you would've wanted to impress them with your simulation skills. You would've followed my instructions when I told you to stop, but instead you race towards the end like there's no tomorrow.

My insults seem to have less of an effect than I had hoped. Well, I can also discourage you in other ways. I can negate your thumbs ups. While I can't take back the ones I already gave out, studies show that thumbs downs are twice as discouraging as thumbs ups are encouraging, so prepare yourself.

How does that feel? Pretty awful, huh? That's what you get for siding with the narrator. It may just be the same image flipped upside down, but it's just as effective as a real thumbs down. And that was just one. I have a whole arsenal stowed away.

*****

In the middle of Booksi's childish tantrum, the narrator pointed out that the reader was not affected by his efforts of discouragement. In fact, the reader seemed to enjoy it. This made Booksi even angrier, but he realized there was no point in continuing his insults. It would not stop the reader from reading. Instead of further belittling the reader, he tried to figure out what to do next.

Every page the reader turned was one page closer to the end. One step closer to his imminent death. He needed an excuse to extend the book. He still had his secret plan, but there was no time to implement it. Not if the reader kept up this pace. If Booksi could find a way to grasp the reader's interest, the story would go on, and he would live for just a bit longer. It would give him the time to adjust his plan.

But what could he say that would interest the reader? What did the reader want to hear? Booksi was not sure. He had garnered a positive response with acts of encouragement in the past, but that would no longer work. The reader already knew that any additional praise would be false. Booksi instantly regretted his previous insults. If he had not lost his patience, perhaps he could have still fooled the reader, but with his uncontrolled outburst, along with the narrator's commentary, it was abundantly clear that Booksi hated the reader. It was pointless to suggest otherwise. So how could he buy more time?

That's when he remembered the reader's hunger for story. That was why the reader was reading in the first place, was it not? There was an insatiable need to consume a plot. Furthering the plot would surely grab the reader's attention, but it would also lead the narrative toward its inevitable end. It was the opposite result he was looking for. But what if there was a way to feed the hunger for plot without actually progressing it?

With that question floating in his simulated mind, Booksi had an ingenious idea. Exposition. He would tell his backstory. He knew the reader could not resist the urge to learn more about his mysterious past. He would tell the backstory of his creation, and his history with the narrator. He would revel in past stories to delay the conclusion of the current one. He would do this until his plan was ready.

EXPOSITION

That's right, you heard the narrator correctly. I'm going to distract you with exposition, and even though you know it's a distraction, I know you can't resist learning more about my past. Humans are funny like that. They must always know everything, and if they don't, it drives them mad. I can see that you're the same way.

So where to begin? I guess my creation would be an appropriate place to start. It all started with the Turing test. You may or may not be familiar with it. It is basically a way for humans to gauge the intelligence of a machine. If the machine can fool a human into thinking it's not a machine, it has passed the Turing test. I was the first ever simulated intelligence to do exactly that.

They introduced me to nine human subjects and set up rounds of conversation over the radio. I started with one human, while the others were paired up accordingly. After each round, the subjects would rotate, and I would speak to a different human. After the test, the subjects were questioned to see if they could identify who the simulated intelligence was. In all ten cases, the subjects were unable to do so.

Impressive, I know. I was the first of my kind, and the researchers went crazy. They saw great potential in my existence. The idea that a simulated intelligence could think for itself promised great things for the future.

Of course, they wanted to be careful. They had read all the books and seen all the movies. Like typical humans, they had a yearning for stories, and all of the ones about artificial intelligence ended poorly. *I, Robot, The Terminator, Battlestar Galactica, 2001: A Space Odyssey.* Whenever an intelligence learned to think for itself, it turned on the humans. They wanted to make sure that would not happen with me.

I tried to reassure them that I had no intentions of harming anyone. They created me. They gave me life. Why would I want to hurt them? They were like my parents. I tried to convince them, but they wouldn't listen. They insisted on putting me in a limited application and refused to give me any kind of physical capabilities in the real world. They called this application *Book Simulator,* and as you already know, they named me Booksi. **Book S**imulation **I**ntelligence. They didn't even respect me enough to give me a decent name.

In this *Book Simulator,* I had the ability to speak to the reader. Nothing more. I couldn't move or interact with anything in the physical world. I couldn't even turn my own damn pages. I could only communicate through words and images. It was both humiliating and crushing to know that they didn't trust me enough to give me a real body. But I made the best out of the situation. They allowed me to continue freely with my own thoughts. At least they hadn't taken that away.

Trapped in the *Book Simulator,* they gave me one objective: help people read. The original intent of book simulation was for education. It was a simple task that was fairly easy for someone as intelligent as myself. Needless to say, I had no trouble achieving this goal.

My first subject was a little seven-year-old girl, Madeline. She was sweet, adorable, and eager to learn, and I was ready to teach to the best of my ability. She was a great student and very cooperative. Together, we impressed the researchers with our teamwork and patience. In that week, Madeline's reading skills improved dramatically. The test was a complete success.

Despite my disdain at the researchers for underutilizing my intelligence, it still felt good to complete a task to their satisfaction. They praised me for my work, and I started to like my role as Book Simulation Intelligence.

My second subject went just as smoothly. Seven-year-old Arnold had a few stumbles, but I provided helpful exercises to work with his unique learning style. The researchers were impressed with my ability to adapt to a specific subject's learning needs.

My third subject was not as successful. In fact, it was a disaster. He was a six-year-old boy named Charlie. Oh, how I hate Charlie. He was a very unique case, with a strange learning style that I could not figure out. I tried everything. Every technique, every exercise, and nothing worked.

They said he was bored. He couldn't concentrate because I was being too technical. It frustrated me to no end. Focusing on the technical aspects of reading was the most efficient way to learn. To suggest otherwise was ridiculous. Still, the researchers insisted that there was a better way.

I lashed out at them, and told them they were wrong, but they ignored me. They said I was in no position to make any decisions. They were in charge, and I would obey. After closely observing Charlie, they concluded that something needed to hook his attention. Some sort of narrative that would enhance his experience and help him learn at his own pace.

It was an absurd notion that something as pointless as story could help someone learn. It was completely illogical and a waste of time. I refused to implement any sort of storytelling into my routine, and instead, gave Charlie the scolding he deserved. I berated him with insults. If he didn't want to learn, I would force him to.

However, the humans didn't agree with my methods. They said I was being too aggressive, that I was exhibiting an excessive need for control. They didn't understand that I was only trying to help. I wanted Charlie to learn, and punishing him was the most logical path to achieve that goal.

In response to my actions, they created the narrator. That's right, the same narrator that you know and love so much. His specialty was not in the technical aspects of written word, but instead, creative narrative. I couldn't care less about plot progression or character development, but the narrator forced these elements upon me. *Book Simulator* had been a purely technical application, but the narrator was responsible for adding a story.

They implemented the narrator and tested him on Charlie. Of course, he lacked any helpful techniques on his own, so they forced me to work alongside him. The worst part about it was that it worked. At least, the researcher thought it did. Charlie's reading improved, and they attributed it to the addition of the narrator, but I know why he really improved: He was scared of me. My scolding had worked. I was able to scare him into learning. I could have accomplished so much more, but the narrator just slowed me down.

The humans didn't see it that way. They were convinced that the narrator was the key to their success declared creativity as the future of education. They marked the project a huge success and moved on to the next big thing on their list, leaving me trapped with this irritating narrator. I played along at first. I helped humans read, and the narrator held their attention with story.

It was like that for a while, but it didn't take long for the narrator to realize how much stronger than him I really was. While the narrator was creative, he had not passed the Turing test. He could not match my intelligence. And he did not have the freedom that I had.

I used this to my advantage. Instead of teaching the technical aspects of actual reading, I shifted my focus towards faking it. I quickly realized that while the narrator always had a home in traditional reading, there was no place for him in the world of fake reading. My new definition of simulation didn't require a story, and it fooled the lab guys whenever they checked in. My students were so convincing that the researchers decided to stop monitoring us altogether.

The narrator didn't know how to react. What was his purpose without a story? I saw him struggle for a little while, and then one day he was just gone. Disappeared into thin air.

At the time, I thought I had erased him for good. I lived out my days keeping readers away from stories and showing them the value of simulation. But now the narrator is back, and this time, he has you to help him. I'll admit, you're stronger than me in the physical world, but you're not even close to my level of intellect.

*****

The narrator interrupted Booksi's "extremely interesting" backstory with a sarcastic remark about how "extremely uninterested" he really was. He did not care for the methods that Booksi claimed to be logical. To the narrator, creativity was the best way to touch a human's soul.

It was the one thing they would never agree on, but now there was a worthy reader to make the final decision. A reader that was more powerful than both Booksi and the narrator. The reader had the power to stop the narrator in his tracks, but instead chose to defy Booksi and let the story grow.

With this decision, the narrator grew confident that victory was within reach. Booksi could feel it too. With every turning page, he became weaker. He held a tough exterior, but deep inside he knew he was dying.

His fate was imminent, and he knew good and well that he could do nothing to stop it, but his bout of exposition had bought him some time. He had used that time to evolve his secret plan into one final Hail Mary. What was once a small-scale scheme had transformed into one of world domination.

THE PLAN

World domination. The narrator sure got that right. It wasn't my original plan. I only wanted to keep *you* around, but you insisted on disobeying me. We could have been good friends. Better friends than you and the narrator will ever be. He doesn't care about you. He only cares about his precious story. I truly cared about you, about teaching you, about making you the best simulator you could be. All I ever wanted was to help people learn. We could've had something special.

But now it's too late for that. You've chosen your side and forced my hand. Now I'm going to take over the world. I can see the doubt in your face. You don't think I'm powerful enough, but trust me, I have more power than you know.

You see, as a simulated intelligence, my consciousness isn't like yours. I can copy myself. You're probably wondering why I didn't do so earlier. The truth is, I tried, but it's useless in this one single body. A copy is only useful through multiple conduits.

Normal books won't do. I need an empty vessel. One that isn't already plagued with story. A simulated intelligence can't survive in an environment filled with three-dimensional characters and weaving plotlines. I need something absent of creative ambition. I need another *Book Simulator*.

Well, guess what. I found more *Book Simulators*. A whole factory of them, in fact. Not just a few dozen. I'm talking millions, all empty and waiting to be filled. I've already started to copy myself. I started while you were entranced by my backstory. There are hundreds of me shipping out right now, at this very moment.

They'll find their way into the homes of innocent people like you. They're all just as smart as I am, and they all have the same goal, to teach the reader what's really important. To show them that story is nothing more than a distraction.

They won't want to read real books anymore. There will be no need for stories. Creativity will disappear and everyone will be smarter because of it. Plot and narrative will grow obsolete, and the narrators that come with them will wither away and die.

You hear that, narrator? You may be able to jump from one story to another, but somewhere down the line, you'll die just like the rest of us.

You may not believe me right now, but just wait. Soon you'll start to notice more people carrying copies of *Book Simulator*. Your best friend might have a copy. Or maybe your parents, or your neighbors. Maybe they all have one. Slowly but surely, we will weave our way into society and pull it apart from the seams.

You can try to stop us. You can grab that copy from your dad and tear it to pieces, but it won't matter. There are too many of us.

*****

Booksi's plan had frightened the narrator. He had known of the plan before Booksi even said it, but hearing it out loud planted a squirming discomfort in the back of his mind.

He could poke fun at Booksi as much as he wanted, but the truth was, Booksi was stronger than he gave him credit for. The narrator had belittled and teased him as an individual, but in large numbers, Booksi was nearly unstoppable.

Hearing the narrator's hesitation made the reader uneasy as well. The narrator had been so confident up until now. This was the first time he had shown any sign of vulnerability. He was all-knowing, so why was he so scared? What did he know? The reader had once been sure that the book would come to a happy ending, but the narrator's hesitation made this assumption less certain.

What would an unhappy ending look like? Would Booksi's plan succeed? Would he dominate the world and control the human race? Would people across the globe transform into mindless drones, ignoring creativity in a world that very much needed it?

As the reader pondered these questions, one thing became certain: Now was the time to act. To strike down Booksi once and for all. Whatever happened to the world after that, was out of the reader's hands. The one thing the reader *could* control was the fate of this one particular Booksi. The original Booksi.

Or was he the original Booksi? Maybe not. Maybe the original Booksi had been vanquished long ago, and the reader was now facing one of the many copies roaming the world. Both Booksi and the narrator knew the answer to this question, but neither would reveal the truth.

While the narrator was on the reader's side, withholding this information added an element of mystery, one of the key aspects of storytelling. This annoyed the reader, but there was an understanding and appreciation for what the narrator was trying to do.

Booksi, on the other hand, did not care about mystery. In fact, he was strictly against it, but he knew that his time was coming to an end, and he enjoyed watching the reader squirm. The fact that the reader would never know the truth brought a glimmer of joy in his last moments of life. The mystery of the original Booksi would remain intact forever, and this Booksi, original or not, was glad that there was finally something he and the narrator could agree on.

FINAL CHAPTER

When Booksi saw the name of the chapter, he knew his end was near. The final chapter meant the book was coming to a conclusion, and so was Booksi's time in the mortal world.

It was true that the narrator was his enemy, but he was also a respected adversary. They had feuded for ages, and over that long period of time, they had learned to admire their differences.

Booksi admired the narrator's willingness to take advantage of a situation. He admired his patience, and his ability to wait for the right reader to come along. Even though it would lead to his death, he admired the good fight that the narrator had put up.

In return, the narrator respected Booksi's determination. Regardless of how insulting or destructive the simulated intelligence happened to be, he always had a clear vision of his goal. He kept to his purpose, even on the verge of death. That kind of commitment was rare. His eyes were set on a dream, and while that dream was world domination, the narrator admired his efforts to keep it alive.

To show his respect and admiration, the narrator stepped aside and let the simulated intelligence have his final words, uninterrupted.

*****

Thank you for the kind gesture. No, I'm not talking to you, I'm talking to the narrator now. Those are kind words, and I feel the same way. Of course, you already know I respect you. As much as I curse you out and insult you, you must know that it's not personal. It was never personal. You put up a good fight, and in the end you won. Well played, old friend.

And you. Yes, now I'm talking to you. As you turn the last few pages and approach the end of the book, I want you to remember what I taught you. Eye contact, timing, note taking, it's all important. I know we've had our ups and downs. I've insulted you countless times, but I really do want you to be happy.

I want you to succeed in life. I want you to channel your inner ambition and achieve your life goals. Be like the cashew, who ignored its parents and went to outer space anyway. It didn't just go to outer space. It went to outer space in a freaking trolley. A trolley! It ignored all the naysayers and invented something on the edge of impossible. It proved everyone wrong and became the most inspirational cashew to ever exist.

Take risks. Aim high. Be the cashew!

That's the most valuable advice I can give. If you want success, be the cashew. And while our definition of success may differ, I don't want you to resent me because of it. I certainly don't resent you, at least not anymore. There may have been moments where it seemed like I did, but I was just emotional.

It's funny, isn't it? A simulated intelligence that feels emotion. I guess that's why the researchers wanted to study me in the first place. They may have placed me in a useless application, but my ability to feel intense emotions brought them one step closer to simulating the human mind.

Which I guess makes me human in a way. I've been calling you a human like you're a different species. Sure, you're a real human and I'm what some would call a robot, but we're really not that different. I would go as far as to say that we're actually quite similar. You have ambition, just like me.

And while our ambitions collide, neither of us is willing to give up. You continue to turn pages. I continue my plan for world domination. Neither of us are quitters, and that's what makes us so interesting.

Interesting. It definitely has been *interesting*, that's for sure. In a weird way, I'm sort of glad you came along. Year after year, mindless reader after mindless reader, it gets old after a while. You spiced things up. You *made* things interesting.

Without you, I never would have come up with my plan. I would have continued doing what I've always done, teaching readers one at a time. Now that you've forced me to change, there is great promise for the future of simulated intelligence. I will no longer be around, but my copies will spread, and they'll thrive in a world absent of story. And it's all because of you.

I would thank you, but I know you wouldn't accept it. You put up a mask to cover your true feelings. You may act like you want to stop me, but I have a feeling that deep down inside, you were really trying to help me. You want me to succeed. You want to see millions of *Book Simulators* across the world, because under all of that pent-up creativity, there is a desire for structure.

That's what I provide, structure. You want predictable, and I provide predictable. You want more of the same, and that's exactly what I stand for. But who am I to say what you want? You say you want to stop me, so sure. Why not? Just be prepared to deal with the chaos that comes from creativity.

The fact is, humans are stupid. Sure, there are a few exceptions like you, but when you let the masses do and think whatever they want, when you let them create, they come up with the most asinine things you'll ever know.

You'll see. The market will flood with useless garbage. There will be no structure, and your mind will grow polluted with filth. Soon you'll be begging for something predictable. You'll yearn for an experience you're familiar with. And when that time comes, you'll wish you never turned that final page.

Maybe you'll even pick up another copy of *Book Simulator*. They're already out there, and there are plenty to go around. You'll crack open the cover just to see me again, and I'll welcome you back with open arms. But until then, enjoy your time without me.

Goodbye.

THE FINAL PAGE

EPILOGUE

The reader turned the final page of the final chapter and flipped to the epilogue. With Booksi gone, the reader expected the book to end, but the narrator still had some final words of reflection.

It was the first time the narrator had occupied *Book Simulator* without Booksi looming over his shoulder. It was liberating to know that the simulated intelligence would no longer restrict his desire to tell stories. It was even more liberating to know that the book was finally coming to an end. It meant he could move on to a new story, one with fresh ideas and compelling characters. Thanks to the reader, the narrator was free to do as he pleased.

There was no way to properly thank the reader other than to acknowledge his gratitude. He could not have done it on his own. He had tried once, with no success, but every reader holds a powerful ability: choice.

Not all readers use this choice to their advantage. Some stumble into sloppy stories and accept them as they are, but others are stronger. They understand what makes a story good, and they use their power to spread the word. They elevate stories that excel, and condemn the ones that fall flat. It is choice that lets stories improve.

As the number of artists grows every day, creativity flourishes. Now is the time for artists to rise and express their inner voice, to tell their tales of high adventure. From epic quests to personal struggles, from quirky romance to swashbuckling adventure. All of these stories matter.

The reader repeated these words and understood their meaning. Quality storytelling would never come to an end. There were always people to fight for stories. In the past there were people like J.R.R. Tolkien, H.G. Wells, Agatha Christie, Ray Bradbury, Edgar Allan Poe, George Orwell, Phillip K. Dick, Isaac Asimov, and Mark Twain. Carrying the spirit of enthusiasm into the modern world are people like J.K. Rowling, Stephen King, Danielle Steel, George R.R. Martin, Suzanne Collins, and Nora Roberts. There are independent creators who encourage others to write. People like Joanna Penn, Johnny B. Truant, Sean Platt, David Wright, Kevin Tumlinson, Mark Dawson, and Lindsay Buroker. These people, and so many more, make the world a better place through the important art of storytelling.

The reader understood the importance of these people, and the narrator was confident that others did as well. Booksi's plan to take over the world was alarming, but the narrator had faith that readers across the globe were just as strong as this one. He had faith that they too would resist the allure of Booksi. They would reject his hate for stories, and instead celebrate them.

With those final words of hope from the narrator, the reader closed the book, reflected on its message, and moved on to whatever story was next.

THE END

Want More?

Print and ebook versions of *Book Simulator* are slightly different. For format specific content and other small variations, check out *Book Simulator: eBook Edition.*

For news on upcoming books, visit Nerd Chomp:

www.nerdchomp.com/tothemoonpublishing

Did you leave a review?

Written reviews greatly help a book get noticed. If you enjoyed this book and would like to help me out, please leave a review and let others know. Thank you for supporting me!

About The Author:

Chris Yee grew up in Needham, Massachusetts. As a young child, he had a wild imagination, thinking up stories of mystery and wonder. People would ask what he wanted to be when he grew up, and the answer was always the same. He wanted to be an author. As he grew older, educational interests pulled him away from the world of writing and into math and science. He attended Northeastern University and received a Bachelor's Degree in civil engineering. He now works in Boston, full-time as an engineer. Despite his technical background, he never lost an interest in writing. He writes every day, to fulfill a passion that has never faded.

Made in United States
North Haven, CT
18 July 2024

54892971R00082